I0820332

DID YOU KNOW?
Sharks

young
reed

DID YOU KNOW?

Sharks

Contents

What is a Shark?	6
Meet the family	8
Fascinating facts	10
Special adaptations	12
Toothy tools	14
What's for dinner?	16
Where do they live?	18
Mermaids and more	20
Sharks and people	22

What is a Shark?

- Sharks are members of the fish family. They are known as **cartilaginous fishes** because their **skeleton is made out of bendy cartilage** rather than hard bone.
- They swim by swishing their **tail** from side to side and steering with their **fins**.
- As with all fishes, sharks are **cold-blooded**.
- Close relatives of sharks include **rays**, **skates** and **guitarfishes**.

Guitarfish.

Ray.

Meet the family

- There are more than **five hundred** different species of sharks in the world.
- Sharks come in a wide variety of sizes, from the **ten-metre-long Whale Shark** to smaller species such as **dogfish sharks** that measure only **twenty to thirty centimetres.**

The huge Whale Shark.

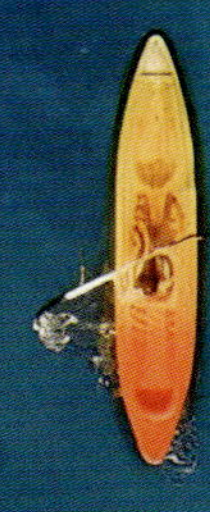

Dogfish.

• Millions of years ago there were much larger sharks. From fossils we know that Megalodon grew up to twenty metres long.

Fossil tooth from a Megalodon and a picture of what the shark would have looked like.

Fascinating facts

Great White Shark.

- The largest living predatory species is the **Great White Shark**, which grows to **seven metres long**.
- It is thought that Greenland Sharks may live for up to **five hundred years**, making them the **longest-lived** vertebrate animals in the world.
- Today's sharks come in a wide variety of shapes, perhaps most famously the weird-looking **Hammerheads**, which use their 'hammer' to **trap stingray prey** against the ocean floor.

Hammerhead.

Greenland Shark.

Special adaptations

- **Thresher Sharks** have extremely long tails, which they use like a **whip** to stun their prey.

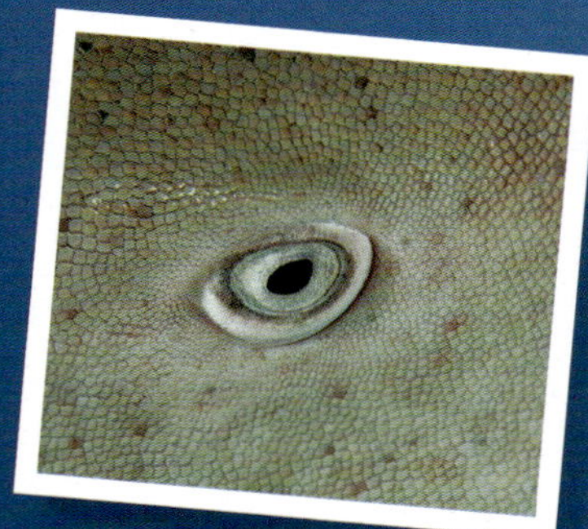

Skin around a shark's eye.

Thresher Sharks.

- Shark **skin** is made up of **dermal denticles**, which are hard tooth-like scales that feel rough like sandpaper.
- Sharks find their prey using super senses – their **hearing** is extremely sensitive and they can **smell** tiny amounts of blood in the water.
- As with other fish, sharks have **gills** that enable them to **breathe** underwater by taking in oxygen.

Shark gills.

Toothy tools

- Sharks grow their **teeth in rows** like a **conveyor-belt** – as one row wears out the next one moves into place.

- Shark teeth come in different shapes and sizes. Some, such as the Great White Shark, have triangular **knife-like** teeth for cutting up big prey.

- Plankton-feeding species, such as Whale Shark and Basking Shark, have **tiny teeth** that are barely used for feeding.

- **Cookiecutter Sharks** have a circle of razor-sharp teeth for cutting a round lump of flesh out of a fish, seal, whale, dolphin, or even another shark!

Cookiecutter Sharks bite out a chunk of flesh from animals such as dolphins.

Kitefin Shark has typical triangular teeth.

Teeth of a plankton-feeding Basking Shark.

Sand Tiger Shark.

What's for dinner?

- Larger sharks are famous for taking **big prey** such as **seals and sea-lions.**
- Some of the **biggest sharks** feed on the **smallest prey** – for example, huge Whale Sharks and Basking Sharks eat only tiny creatures such as plankton.
- Many sharks have a diet focused mainly on eating **other fishes.**
- Bonnethead Sharks sometimes feed on **plants such as seagrasses**, meaning that they are **omnivores** – feeding on both plants and animals.

Great White Shark chasing a seal.

Many shark species feed on other fish.

Plankton viewed through a microscope.

Bonnethead Shark.

Where do they live?

- Sharks live in all sorts of habitats in the sea, with many species living in **deep-water** ocean environments.
- Other species live in shallow waters, resting on **sandy bottoms** or **coral reefs**.
- Sharks live in **oceans all around the world** – they are absent only from the coldest waters near the Arctic and Antarctic.
- A few shark species, such as Bull Sharks and River Sharks, can live in **fresh water**.

Wobbegongs are adapted for camouflage in coral-reef habitats.

Whale Sharks live in tropical seas, both in deep water and on reefs.

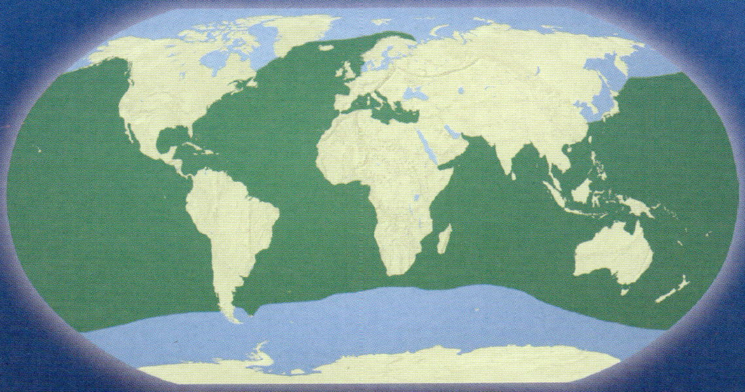

Mermaids and more

- Many sharks are rather **solitary** – the male and female pair up only briefly to mate.
- In some shark species the babies grow in the **mother's womb**, rather like humans and other mammals, while in other species the young develop in eggs.
- Shark eggs are laid in a tough **egg case** known as a **mermaid's purse** – empty ones can often be found washed up on beaches.

An empty 'mermaid's purse' picked up on a beach (left) and an active shark's egg with a baby developing inside.

• When a young shark is born or hatches from an egg, the **baby** that emerges is like a **miniature version** of the adult. They are **independent from birth** and have to fend for themselves.

Leopard Sharks pairing up.

A young Hammerhead – a mini version of the adult.

Divers can watch large carnivorous sharks in the wild using a shark cage.

Sharks are a popular attraction at aquariums.

Sharks and people

- Some of the larger shark species can be **dangerous to humans**, perhaps mistaking us for typical prey items such as seals.

- Most sharks are harmless to humans – each of the five hundred species has a **vital role to play** in the **ocean ecosystem**.

- There are many places around the world where you can **swim with sharks** and watch these amazing creatures in the wild.

- **Hunting by humans** for food, or for shark fins, or just for 'sport', has brought some shark species close to the brink of **extinction**.

Fishing for sharks.

First published in 2025 by New Holland Publishers
Sydney

newhollandpublishers.com

A record of this book is held at the National Library of Australia.

ISBN 9781760798017

OTHER TITLES IN THE 'DID YOU KNOW?' SERIES:

Dolphins
ISBN 9781760798000

Kangaroos
ISBN 9781921073861

Koala
ISBN 9781921073878

Lizards
ISBN 9781921073885

Meerkat
ISBN 9781921073892

Monkeys
ISBN 9781760798031

Penguins
ISBN 9781921073908

Red Panda
ISBN 9781921073915

Tigers
ISBN 9781760798024

For details of these books and hundreds of other Natural History titles see newhollandpublishers.com